Thea Astley: Selected Poems

First published 2017 by University of Queensland Press
PO Box 6042, St Lucia, Queensland 4067 Australia
uqp.com.au
uqp@uqp.uq.edu.au

Cover and text design by Sandy Cull, gogoGingko
Typeset in Adobe Garamond Pro 11.5/14 pt by Post Pre-press Group, Brisbane
Printed in Australia by McPherson's Printing Group, Melbourne

 The University of Queensland Press is supported by the Queensland Government through Arts Queensland.

  The University of Queensland Press is assisted by the Australian Government through the Australia Council, its arts funding and advisory body.

Cataloguing-in-Publication Data
National Library of Australia
Astley, Thea, 1925–2004, author.
Thea Astley: selected poems.
Australian poetry.
Taylor, Cheryl, 1945–, editor.
ISBN 978 0 7022 5979 1 (pbk)
ISBN 978 0 7022 6058 2 (pdf)
ISBN 978 0 7022 6059 9 (epub)
ISBN 978 0 7022 6060 5 (kindle)

Thea Astley

Selected Poems

EDITED BY
Cheryl Taylor

UQP

CONTENTS

Introduction by Susan Wyndham   1

Section I: Childhood and Youth   **5**
Childhood   9
High school poetry, 1939 to 1942   11
Wartime Brisbane, 1943 to 1944   19
Melbourne visit, January 1945   51
Brisbane, 1945   55
Translations from French   77
1946   81
Section II: Adulthood   **87**
Astley's unpublished collection   91
Occasional poems   137

Editor's afterword   145
Editor's biography   150
Editor's acknowledgements   151

Endnotes   152
Index of titles   161
Index of first lines   163

It didn't occur to me that I'd be a novelist. I wrote poetry.

Thea Astley

(Interview with Suzanne Lunney, 1974)

Introduction

SUSAN WYNDHAM

My mother was first to recognise the famous author Thea Astley at the next table in a Sydney café with her son, Ed, and soon Astley was leaning forward like an old friend. I wanted to say how her recent book *Vanishing Points* had moved and entertained me while I was living in New York: her machete-sharp portrait of tropical Queensland, peopled by environmental vandals and escapees from 'progress', explained why I left Australia and why I returned. But Astley was impervious to praise, preferring to swap proud-mother stories and ask questions.

God (as she would say), she was a great Australian.

By the time I interviewed her almost a decade later, in 2003, Astley had stopped writing. 'My writing hairs have worn off with age, like the hairs on your legs,' she said, the one-liners curling out of her mouth through clouds of cigarette smoke and crackling laughter.

She had planned to stop after *Coda*, her 1994 book about an old woman who was 'losing her nouns'. However, the offer of a Creative Fellowship from the Keating government urged her on to write *The Multiple Effects of Rainshadow* and *Drylands*;

the latter shared the Miles Franklin Literary Award in 2000. She was at her best until the end.

Astley more than earned her elevated place in Australian literature, with sixteen novels and short story collections published since 1958 and a haul of prizes that included four Miles Franklins. Much of her writing was done while she taught full-time, raised Ed, and moved restlessly with her husband up and down the coast of Queensland and New South Wales.

What most people did not know was that she had been writing for far longer. From her childhood in Brisbane until she turned to prose in her thirties, Astley poured her emotions, her observations of nature and people, and her feeling for language and metaphor into hundreds of poems. Her output is revealed in Karen Lamb's 2016 biography, *Thea Astley: inventing her own weather*, and more fully in this selection.

A few poems were published, sometimes under the pseudonym Philip Cressy, which gave her cover and earned a man's payment of five guineas instead of a woman's three from *The Sydney Morning Herald*. But much of it was a private self-education.

Even the soul-searching juvenilia is polished by Astley's precocious reading and self-conscious imitation of classical and Romantic poets. Here are landscapes and weather that express human moods. Here are her passion for music and men, her anxiety – 'Tortured by fears of my own making' – and lapsed-Catholic guilt.

As she refines her art, there are glimpses of the satirical novels to come. The Astley voice begins to emerge – confident, flamboyant and as grown-in-Queensland as 'the mango trees all pointilliste'.

And then, just like that, she gave it up. Perhaps her poetry hairs had worn off, or she simply needed more expansive narratives for the screwballs and underdogs who fascinated her and for her 'selfish way of writing out things that worried me'.[1]

The novels came fast and, for better and worse, her early fiction had an abstract lushness that linked her with the 'prose poets' led by her hero Patrick White. With time her sentences became leaner and she reached beyond personal experience into the historical wounds and politics of her country.

Her final work, *Drylands*, was partly self-portrait, partly a eulogy to her beloved northern Queensland in the time of Pauline Hanson, and dedicated to 'the world's last reader'. The protagonist, a middle-aged aspiring writer, dismisses her attempts at poetry that parody Astley's own: 'The pretentiousness of it all!'

Astley never lost her sense of humour and timing. A year after my interview she was a guest at the Byron Bay Writers' Festival and read an old story about the trials of travel, 'Diesel Epiphany', to an audience that rocked with laughter at her deadpan comic performance.

That is how many remember Astley, who died suddenly two weeks later, on the brink of turning seventy-nine.

Ambitious, sensitive to slights, she often complained about inadequate recognition for her work. But she was rightly celebrated as 'a trailblazer' by a New South Wales Premier's lifetime award in 2002. And now, with this selection of poems, we can appreciate the full arc of her brilliant career.

SECTION I

Childhood and Youth

Interviewed in 1990, Thea Astley dismissed 'poetry in adolescence' with characteristic humour as 'a form of acne – I think I'm having a poem'. Yet Astley's poems show that from age fourteen onwards she regarded poetry-writing not only as an emotional release but also as an art that she could work at and perfect.

Two school exercise books in The University of Queensland's Fryer Library contain most of Astley's surviving poetry. Section I exemplifies poems preserved in the earlier book, named here for clarity Exercise Book A.[2] The texts are as Astley hand-wrote or typed and pasted them. Many poems in Exercise Book A were first printed in school and university magazines. They document Astley's development as a poet from 1939 to 1946 – a story of her increasing competence in handling words and techniques, and of her increasing awareness of the untruths that are inherent in a purely romantic view of the world.

Teachers at All Hallows' School encouraged Astley to write. Her participation in the *Barjai* group of young poets and artists and her reading at The University of Queensland of English, French and Latin poets further advanced her poetic skills. 'Absent' (20), Astley's earliest surviving sonnet, foreshadows her continuing interest in traditional forms, which was fostered by her conviction that to succeed poetry had to be more than an effusion of feeling.

While the chaotic feelings associated with love are nevertheless the main subject of Astley's earlier poems, 'Idiot' (26), written when she was nineteen, satirises love conventions themselves. Poems such as 'Toni's' (64) and 'A woman sat beside me in the train' (32) are snapshots of life in wartime Brisbane, while 'With Evening' (30) and '"Look", sang the boy' (24) meditate on the human condition itself, '[c]hained to a tottering world'.

Childhood

At the Seaside

Christopher Robin hand in hand
Ran with his sister along the sand
As on they ran, from close behind,
There came a bark
From big dog Spark.
With big brown eyes and jolly face
He chased them up and down the place.
Good dog Spark gave up the chase
And went home after his happy race.[3]

High school poetry

Astley attended All Hallows' School in Brisbane's Fortitude Valley, where the teaching staff nurtured her literary talents and ambition.

Dreaming

It's pleasant to dream and lie
Lazily, under a summer sky,
And watch the clouds drift slowly by,
And hear the birds in the tree just near,
Their lovely song sounding clear
On the hot still air,
And the sun comes dancing through the tree
On my dreams – and me.

It's pleasant to dream and rest
Quietly, while all the west
(As it calls to the sun with its burning crest),
Flares fiery red shot deep with gold.
And the trees stand out, black and bold
And the air is becoming chilly and cold.
Then the sun's last rays come through the tree
On my dreams – and me.

It's pleasant to dream and sleep
While the sky is turning dark and deep,
And the shadows start to creep.
Then the first, small star begins to wink
As all the red and gold and pink
Fade and die as the sun starts to sink,
And the night folds round in a soft, black sea –
Round my dreams – and me.[4]

Unrest

I find no solace in the haunting days
That creep so slowly by;
Nor in the cool black scarf of night's pathways,
Nor in the sky
So calm, serene …
It has no knowledge of my twisted soul
Seeking peace in vain;
Tortured by fears of my own making –
Fancies of a fevered brain.
I seek to fill my mind with other thoughts,
A tree, a limpid pool, an evening sky,
Striving to find comfort in their grace.
But all this sorrow unexpressed by sigh,
Will wreck my soul, will spoil, will mar, will break.
My heart is like a bird trapped in a cage,
With no escape.[5]

Fantasy

My thoughts have borne me far –
And so I'll stay; in an eternity
Of wisdom. Guided as if by a star
To where all things of beauty and of goodness are.
And with an age of quiet I am wrapped around,
And peace is come upon me.
For beauty is in every flowering thorn,
In every lake; and but the murmuring sea
Shall stir a vibrant thought – shall form an everlasting memory.
Thus have I been carried, drifting on the lake
Of dreams, and fantasy has beckoned me away
My thoughts have borne me far –
And so I'll stay.[6]

The Awakening

Unloose the golden bars of dawn
Across the sky.
And bathe the sombre clouds
In rosy hue; let fly
A brilliant banner in the morn
Glinting in rubies on the dewy grass,
Outlining gilt around the clouds that pass
Slowly up from the sun.
Send forth, O Dawn, your heralds. Come
To the day from the prison of the night,
And in soft colours steep the fields
Drowsy in the misty light.
Let all your glory be unfurled
Once more unto the [f]ight.

Enchantment

Pale sky, unto thy heart let me be gathered
     Drinking deep your dreams
Let me be untethered
Freed to fly to thee
     A lark to the sun,
Strangely remote from earth, and strangely one
     With shadowy fantasy.
Unto thine arms let me but come
     To rest.

For the burning sky of eve
     Has made my heart
A captive bird, a leaping fire
     Aflame to pant
These sleepy dales, and leave
     Behind
The earth; cannot a wind
     Twirl me higher,
Higher a little than the highest hill?
     Bending to me,
Thine arms should lift me still
     Unto thee.

May I not sing with thee, O sky, thy song,
     Sweet as life and long
As life is long?
     Touch my lips with its everlasting breath.
     To me
     In thee

There is no death.
Smiling eager do I come to thee –
Unto thy heart thou hast gathered me.[7]

To You – The Poet

You stood apart from others – weaver of dreams,
For your soul found joy in the light of a star;
You felt with pain the splendour of a hill,
Or your spirit went flying afar,
Caught in a mad delight in the screaming wind
That lashed white on the grey of the sea.
You knew, too, the sorrows of men,
All the care that can be.

I have seen you gaze on a stream, your eyes filled with delight
At the slow-moving ripples that weave
Their way through the reeds. There can be no sight
But it fills you with joy or with pain;
You breathe dreams and live them. Again,
As you watched the last ragged autumn-leaf falling,
Or the first fragrant bloom of spring,
You mourned with the tear-furrowed wrinkles of age,
You rejoiced with the laughter of youth –
Such emotions can these things bring.
And I saw, as you looked on a sun-dappled vale,
Your joy – and your sight dimmed with tears;
And I gazed in your eyes to see …
The dreams of a thousand years.[8]

Wartime Brisbane

1943 TO 1944

Astley continued to publish poems in *All Hallows'* *magazine* for three years after she graduated from the school in November 1942. Poems such as 'Grey Afternoon' (29) and 'A woman sat beside me in the train' (32) capture Brisbane's subdued tones during the anxious years of World War II. Other poems written in this period proved to be a starting point for her fiction's searching analyses of sexual relationships.

Absent

You are not here today so I must find
Pictured upon that page, your smile, your eyes.
And seeing, feel a thousand sorrows rise
To mourn you fled. Can I not capture, bind
Your soul unto this leaf? Or shall I, blind,
Seek in the shadowy semblance, all that lies
Of fair within reality? – Whilst sighs
Like white-winged birds flock through my mind.

Then from the phantom seas of swirling thought
You come, and all the mists are flung apart.
My hands stretch out to welcome you long sought!
I soar on wings of star-bound ecstasy.
And feel a sudden singing in my heart –
Far from the page your eyes smile back at me.[9]

The Shadows

My room is patterned with leaves,
My heart with song
And phantom wonder weaves
A quivering spell
Of tangled leaf and light
While sweet and long
A bird sings, and the haunted, dumb walls tell
Its gleaming flight,
Lost in a world of shade where I am part.
For leaves have captured my walls –
And song my heart.

I turn to the window – the trees
The waking green
And then to my walls – a frieze
Of dreaming grey
And warmly glowing gold.
The half-unseen
Stories that in the moving shadows play
At plots grown old,
Touch my heart into flame and wild thoughts throng.
My room is patterned with leaves –
My heart with song.[10]

From Troy

For Oenone

Sing of the sunset sky, the strange chill plains
Of pallid evening; the wings
That passing, make a music murmuring low.
Sing of the golden love
That mocked the night of woods,
Where Ida sang the love of woman's heart.

For Helen

Sing of the flashing trees, the starlit night,
With wonder from the shrouded years
Up-shooting through the liquid centuries.
Sing of the golden flame
That mocked the night of woods,
Where Ida cursed the love of woman's heart.[11]

To Laurie [1]

You have a slow smile
That breaks the solemn dreamings of your eyes,
That builds a subtle mystery round your lips.
Cool replies
Float from you like bright ships'
Sails sweeping ice-blue waters in your eyes.

When you are cold with iron in your thoughts
And lips are smooth with unwarmed wonderings,
I court
A smile and my own brings
A warmth to those blue waters, flooding thought
Within a slow smile.[12]

Poem [1]

'Look,' sang the boy,
'A pillar burning white
'With sculptured flowers at its head,
'Pregnant omens of the dead
'Scentless in the night!'

'Look!' called the girl,
'A lily pale in flame,
'Its silver flesh a quivering spire
'Transitioned from cold clay to fire
'As subtle darkness came.'

'Look!' they all cried,
'A crumbling mast of stone,
'A withered flower upon the grass,
'A lifeless moon and stars of glass,
'And coldness in the bone.'

'No!' cried the boy.
'No!' sang the girl.
'See the shadows hurled
'With windy cloaks like swelling waves
'About us – we, at midnight, slaves,
'Chained to a tottering world!'[13]

Creation

This must be part of my making –
The loneliness, no love! No love!
For all thoughts find their waking
Mere abstractions, passionless above
The vibrant strings of human dreams –
With no song breaking.
And I have learned the language of the stars,
And found a truer note in life awaking.

But there will be a breaking
Of cold steel cords. As sudden fire
Will brush my heart and cheek;
A white carved spire
Of pale ideals will crumble down. I seek
The warmth and true humanity
Will come, a sleepy sun with heat in waking,
Tempering the steel …
And I – I am become a man!
But O God! The pain in the making![14]

Idiot

He picked a rose
And cupping thin young hands,
Crooned over it with little laughing cries;
Pressed with hyperbolic gesture
The bright thing to his mouth
And brushed its softness slowly on closed eyes.
The great ones laughed.
Red anger coiled his heart.
He tore the petals, stripped the green stalk bare –
And crushed them red beneath his heel …
Then stricken raised his head,
And smiled a vacant smile to the soft air.[15]

Love's Fault

Not yet have I stumbled upon a philosophy
For you are of iron, of leaf and of song
No logic can capture your lips or belong
To your eyes;
Or find realisation when your light desires
Blow me a tree in the wind of your song.
Not yet a philosophy.

I am whipped by your hair, by its heart-scourging rope,
(For you are of steel, of leaf and of song);
A puppet to love and caught in your strong
Lovely hands
No thought can concur with your fickle demands,
So I bend to your iron, kiss your leaf, sing your songs,
Not yet a philosophy.

Query

Tell me dear, how long
In this long day
Our hearts winged on together.
The autumn leaves are wrong
To blow our way.
We must catch and tether
Scarlet leaves on sodden trees,
Running shades on slender grass,
Nothing must escape –
For we are fleeing; now love sees
That we are come as leaves to trees.

Grey Afternoon

Limpid afternoon, water-light
With missing values on the clouds,
Grey smoke sky-traced by trains; ghost crowds
Blurring through cold streets in half-born night.

A river shaking greyness of the fields
To life with dark green on their breast,
And over it to a sunless west,
Pigeons floating where the half light yields.

Grey are the shadows drifting on the skies,
Grey the chimney-stacks, the birds,
Grey the city spires, the words
I spoke to you. And grey, my dear, your eyes.

With Evening

With evening the city was lost in an ocean
Of purple-grey silences; people were shades
Slipping by into darkness. And I – oh I
Was a pale little ghost.

Stars were pinned to steeples; in the streets
Night flowed its deep rivers, where traffic gleamed by,
Strange fish in strange waters; and shrilly the cry
Of a paper-boy stabbed through the ear of the night.

> The little houses were silent.
> The sneering lips of the lanes
> With sinister pools of lamplight
> Splashed along their blackness
> Were waiting …

Along the gutter a boy playing marbles
Was chattering softly, half-drowned in the shadow.
And thought came gnawing the clay of my mind,
That I was a child in the wind of life;
Recognition of worlds as a few coloured balls
That I prodded at will with my thumb.

> We were all waiting –
> The stars, the small houses, the lanes
> That were crookedly grinning –
> The whole world expectant of moon-rise.
> But the boy was still clicking his marbles,

Flicking them blindly,
And my lips twisted into thin laughter
As I ran past the smug little doorways,
Leaving them waiting.

Poem [2]

A woman sat beside me in the train,
July the seventeenth of forty-four
And strange remarks fell from us like soft rain.
'Oh once I saw,'
She said, though we had never met before,
Swaying her plaited head towards the door,
'Fields of daffodils,
'And forests autumn-painted angry hills,
'Slopes blue with flowers, white with snow.'
I do not know
If she were dreaming swaying by the door,
But her words were subtle sorrows.
'Life has tried me; now the cold days gnaw
'My heart, my heart.
'What magic part
'Of earth's philosophy may yet remain
'For me?' – questioningly swaying as before,
She who sat beside me in the train.
'Even sunlight borrows
'Shadows from the night.' But no replies
Bloomed in me. I was lost within her eyes
Though we had never met before.
And O the pain
That flooded as I parted from the train
And sharply saw
Her plaited head bent backwards from the door,
Swaying, swaying, as it had before.

Sonnet: Child by the Shore

Under strange seas of sky to a stranger sea
White shell of a child, you blew, foam-sprung, and blown
The paleness of you, slightness of you sown
Into grey ripples, tree-like subtlety
About the hair; your limbs an imagery
Of leaping spray. While round you, long gulls flown
To capture silver fish, found suns unknown
Gleaming where your feet splashed dazzlingly.

　　The evening swept shadows on the day;
　　The yellow dunes humped on late afternoon.
　　And you were a mistiness in light's decay
　　Still singing with the sea. And then I saw
　　Your shadow long and black beneath the moon,
　　As the waves came creeping, creeping on the shore.

Sonnet: Frustration

Sun-flash on water, perhaps a writhing fire
Among the dark reeds of my windy thought?
Or were you a moon? I chased your gleam and caught
A winter coldness weaved about a spire
Made from your subtle laughters – they, a pyre
Where with dagger leaves my passion fought
To break your stone, reached for you, madly sought
Solution to your song that would not tire.

> Swans on the river slept, but all the years
> Crept on us watching, sneering lips and eyes.
> And O my heart was dead in its own fears,
> Leaf-tossed from your light upon a breath –
> Leaving me cold flesh beneath the skies –
> A cynic toying with the thought of death.

Sonnet: To Francis Thompson

Your words have spun eternity – and did
You love to toss the stars as you tossed phrases? –
Wandering through intricacies of mazes
Built upon the syllables you bid?
Eager I wandered with you, with you hid
From all the subtle laughters, sudden crazes
Of this wind-flung world; and in the hazes
Of your warm dreams, found my sorrow rid.

> Singer, I know the places that *you* knew,
> But your words hang a pathos in the air,
> Heavy as great birds winging. Years subdue
> The fleshly agonies – but thought condemns
> That with grey water I must see you there –
> When you – dear God! – sold matches by the Thames.[16]

Sonnet: To Myself

You are the one who many years before
When trees were white with bloom among the hills,
Wandered the scented paths – and in the stills
Of purple valleys learned the warm earth's lore –
And found for each new dream a hundred more.
O heart so full of ghosts – as passion fills
The brain with spectre shapes which logic kills –
Time has torn the mists that once you wore!

      For now you gather blossoms from the air,
      And pungent scents with no reality;
      Capture laughter creeping down the stair
      Of dying thought; revive in haunted sleep
      A fragile past – while as in mockery,
      A dim form comes with sickle poised to reap.

To Helen

Only an hour or so my friend – then pass
Me quickly the hot wine of your thoughts.
The glass
So tilted to my lips is sweet;
And I am drunk with song upon your tongue –
But wings are on your feet.

Flood the brief pulsing minutes with the throb
Of sharply-carven joys and shaded tears.
The sob
Of memory is in my heart
But see how swiftly time's two fingers stir –
Move us, like them, apart![17]

Sonnet: Chance Meeting

This day has been a season out of place,
Summer greenness rising from the dust
Of winter's heart; a memory-sharpened thrust
Of time's slim finger. Through the chain-locked space
Where world chased little world, I caught the face
Predestined by the year to break the crust
That winter built about the spring. (They must,
Those memories, tortured in grim time's embrace!)

    The little sulking streets bloomed into lanes.
    An echoed spring shook leaves upon bare trees,
    While soul and flesh merged into joy that strains
    The tongue to words. Through this, command has come,
    When summer burns to autumn's subtleties,
    July will sing, September will be dumb.[18]

Sonites

Summer is sweetness
And sweetness is singing,
As the strange incompleteness
Of bells that cease ringing.
And singing is laughter,
But laughter is shadow
Creeping and crying,
The wavy green meadow
Where dreamers come flying.
Shadow is sorrow,
While sorrow is parting,
And parting tomorrow
Means salty tears starting.
So summer is sadness,
While sweetness is keeping –
A lamentable madness,
Paradoxical weeping.[19]

Meditation

(From the French of Baudelaire)

Be wise, O my Sorrow, and calmer tread your way.
You plead for night; it falls and swift is here,
The town is wrapped in atmosphere of grey,
Bringing peace to some – to others care.
While the base multitude of mortals course
Under Pleasure's tyrant-wielded blows
To cull in slavish festival, remorse,
My Sorrow, give me your hand and find repose

Far from them. See the dead years bending down
The balconies of sky in ancient gown.
Smiling Regret surge from deep waters waste,
Beneath an arch the dying sun finds its bed.
And like a young shroud trailing to the East,
Hear, beloved, hear the sweet Night tread.[20]

For the Pleasure of Laurie

When I am dead and little blades of grass
Lap round my grave as in a shallow sea,
You will know the sorrow of the years –
Because of me.

And though the flesh be parted from the flesh,
The future is predestined, and you must
Shed a tear or two, and haunted see
Seven lilies blooming from my dust.[21]

Revelation

Enter – harshness,
The facing of the world.
And you who say you love me,
Wanton, hurled
Your pretty little love-arts to the air
And said – 'There –
'Love is cheap, and I have a little money.
'Buy me a brazen word or two
'And dip in honey.
'Press
'With a caress,
'My sweetened offerings of bliss,
'And swear eternally
'To one.'
Meanwhile between this and the kiss,
You boast of other women you have caught,
Then come to me,
And swear with eager eyes
That you are the ardent seeker
I, the only prize![22]

String Quartet

Four fiddlers by the shaded lamp,
And yellow glow
Upon the polished wood,
And bow,
A silver flash across the strings.

Ravel has chords of mystery blue
And passages that follow
Like rain, to flood the hollow
Of the tensely waiting hall.
Fall, fall,
Notes on the wind of a passionate bow,
And lamps will flicker, blow
To a gusty darkness,
While out of the blackened stage,
Screaming, the bows will rise
To a tempest rage,
And then, as suddenly droop to a whimpering sigh,
Holding a hundred hearts to one, while song abating,
Leaves the hollows soundless and sad,
And the great hall nervously waiting.[23]

Song [1]

When shivering roses fade in sleep,
And sleep is a whitened sorrow,
Love is a dream, and deep,
Deep is the pain on the morrow.

Hills carved clean by a bitter wind
May tearless stay, but lovers borrow
All of their pain and find,
Deep is regret on the morrow.

Roses and hills unlamented depart,
But departure of love is a gall-tasting sorrow,
Locking the walls of the heart,
To the vagabond sun on the morrow.

Trellis

Where wind wanders round the curtains,
Shaking the dead grey light of six o'clock,
The bright hair dulls, and the thin hand whitens
Cold on the sill. And strained eyes coldly seek

The white-wood pattern of the trellised wall.
Under and over with the black leaves,
Cross on cross on cross the charmed eyes trail
To mental crucifixion with the bleak leaves.[24]

To Isa

We met (a quiet street) within the town today,
The pleasure in her eyes lit fires in mine.
Old oaks threw purple shade along the footpath way,
And memory drugged the air like scented wine.

We talked and found a story made for every name,
Tilted the glass and slowly sipped our wine,
Paced slowly through dreams and parted whence we came –
The sorrow in her eyes found tears in mine.

Poem [3]

Beyond the sleeping and the wake,
Beyond the dying and the birth
Of light and dark, where small things take
To slender wings from shadowed earth;
Where shade and substance part –
There goes the heart.

To the dreaming I confide
As little towns are merged with dusk,
The pulsing of my heart's red tide
Dissevered from a withered husk.
But where the flesh and sorrow meet –
There run my feet.[25]

Song [2]

Eheu, fugaces, Postume, Postume
Labuntur anni
    —Horace

Quick, love, snatch the curtains from the years,
The crazy figure smiting out the hours
Upon old fears
Of iron solidity
Is unaware of us. Red flowers
Are in your hair. Philosophy
Is weak before your eyes,
So quick love, snatch the curtains from the years.

The night is trembling for past centuries
As *your* lips tremble for remembered song.
New sophistries
Are slain by the shadow of a rose,
Mythologies have life, and pale gods throng
The hill as they might Greece. Love blows
Us back. Sweet, can you see
The sun on Plato's head, hear Sophocles?

I have your hand as we flee back through time –
Two children seeking a forgotten kiss
As befooled moths will climb
Towards their pyre of light.
But hours pound on with crazy emphasis
Upon the languid eye-lid of the night.
Draw back the curtains, love,
And leave our phantom kisses in a rhyme.[26]

Poem [4]

I said:– 'O look at the trees!'
And we ran to the little gate,
Watching the twist of the road,
'See the moonlit subtleties
'Lurching to where we wait
'Near the eyes of the little gate.'

I pleaded:– 'Dance with the wind!'
And we fled down the moonlit lane
Where the sea of green trees flowed.
But the small gate wickedly grinned,
And whispered 'Never again'
As we fled down the leaf-dappled lane.

I asked:– 'Can you see that star?'
And we craned by the tenement wall
Where the street lamp shadows strode.
'Oh we have journeyed far
'To see a dead star fall
'On our hearts by a tenement wall.'

Sonnet [1]

Beyond this year – the unknown corridor,
The years ahead. Beyond this heart – the place
Where still the heart will go – and there the face
That smiles now at my own. O I implore
The obliviscence of today – no more
Than that, but that my feet will always race
Your shadow, and your shadow find no trace,
But hear the closing of a distant door.

There where the doubtings of this comic hour
Are swept into the dust-bin of forced laughter,
I hope to banish you till years devour
Your image, and love cuts its little whips,
Yet who knows but I shall pause as you run after,
To know the sudden terror of your lips.[27]

Melbourne visit

The three poems following indicate that Astley and her parents travelled to Melbourne in January 1945 to visit her brother Philip, who was in training as a Jesuit at the Loyola Seminary in Watsonia (now Loyola College).

To My Brother

Sunlight and spires are strangely tangled
With plane trees and elms in a Monday memory
Of fat brown horses, listless waiting
And laughter waltzing from a woman's lips.

You were the serious one who gravely
Listened to snatches of dreamy Debussy
And arrow-like echoes from old Lamartine,
Smiling the moments away in a prayer;

Fathomless, even. But this day remembers
Your feet on the pavement of three people's hearts,
Strangely confused with a cold rain and elms,
And a red-headed child in a sunlit street.[28]

Poem [5]

Boringly repetitive the night
Takes up the tale, and streets reveal
Lamp-posts polished by the moon to steel,
Elms of ebony and fences white –
Gaspingly unreal.

Eyes and lips and lips and hair become
Ash-grey daubings. Breath and bone
Chilled, magic-killed, can now disown
The sun's disquietudes and moon-mad-numb,
Repress day with a groan.[29]

Melbourne

The long long hours of afternoon
Obliquely lie across the brow
Pressing lids to darkness, sun
And sleep upon the hair move slow

To darkness, ashen-grey at first
And then a fluid, beating black
As heated, primed, the red sun bursts,
And splintered gold burns slowly out.[30]

Brisbane

1945

In 1945, the year she turned twenty, Astley attended Kelvin Grove Teacher's College by day and second-year Arts studies at The University of Queensland in the evenings.

Shorncliffe

The crouching houses turn their moon-splashed sides
To the calling shore. Softly the moon
Slips past my window pane and frightened hides
From the peering earth and tugging tides
Of windy June.

Communicative trees may hear the cry
That bursts from white lips parted in the dark,
But brief lovers like the moon make no reply.
The taut soul, barren, gazes with damp eye
Across the park.[31]

The Card Players

Lamp-flicker on the bending men
Whose gnarled hands palm the frowning kings
And sullen knaves, creates again
Four shadow players, hugely brings

Their acts to screening on the wall,
And hovering black above the cards
The shadows swell and swell and fall,
Watching on like restless guards.

Duplicated, one hand claws
A coat, and thinking dark deceives,
The shadow sharper quickly draws
A card from up a shadow sleeve.[32]

Roland to Arlène

My dearest lady,
You are all the day and night I wish to know
Entity of thought and heart complete
In thought and heart of you. Now new streams flow
My love-ship to the dark lakes of your eyes
Calmer than a land where winds blow
And cut the still of your soul's retreat
With flashing sails and sharply curving bow.
O let me anchor safely in your heart
For roaming your eyes' seas is very sweet,
But even sad Ulysses found a woe
In endless pattern and perplexity
Of oceans never-ending. See, I weep.[33]

Vignette

Light this branch at the moon,
And gild the air
With it. In ritual
Unloose your hair.

I shall clutch by handfuls,
Stars saffron – cold
For powdering your dark head,
Black-burnt-gold.

Then bind your locks as mine.
See, one by one
The stars slip from the sky –
The mime is done.[34]

Returned Man

Take back the day.
For scarlet flowers and lean grass in the wind
Are tainted with this fear that carves a way
Of night into the noon. My sorrow, grinned
At, hears the long screams of the men, and runs
In terror, hearing still the guns.

And take the night,
Now that the moon is bitter as a curd;
For all the days don darkness in their spite.
Here no wanting. Offered but the word,
The plea for nullity; too dried to weep
The heart begs time leave only sleep.[35]

The Sailor

His eyes were full of holy things.
But the tongue was still.
And only tongued waves grumbled round the boy,
And licked his boots and hands.
Then down the hill
Across the stripy sands,
Faces, figures, gabbling lips and feet
Came moving – massed like clouds on windless days,
Gathered and pressed and all their bird-like hands
Touched with light fingers,
Swept back the greenly curving strands
Salt-spattered weeds. And then they made
A repetitious chorus, sounds
That shook the shags from wrinkled rocks
To feathered foam –
A chorus-storming of his name …
But his eyes were full of holy things,
And no words came.
So lifting him and bearing him
Down stripy shore and up brown hill,
They tracked the lone wastes of the evening sky,
Moving like a cloud above the hill.
And he lay quietly as if wings
Light-lifted him, the white lips still
And his eyes were full of holy things.[36]

Altar Piece

Sleekly the marble holds them
In a future made the present,
Pasts that never are –
Shallow carvings brinked upon fruition
Of an act of adoration;
Puzzled Peter, hands upraised,
And John upon his breast.
He. And cunning midst the carven faces,
A carven scorn within his beard,
Judas, in the sea of faces
Frozen into marble wonder,
Simulating wonder like the rest,
Around the sacrificial table,
Watches the uplifted bread …
All whitely silent through the year,
Each stone figure brinked on action,
Christ about to breathe a prayer,
And James about to bow his head.[37]

The Unwanted

'Because perplexed me people's laughter, words
'Rocketing and rioting about
'The heart, in valleys now huge grins, and birds
'In flocks shafts raining, each day doubt,'

Pleaded the fool, poised by the sea's dark jaw,
Death minded to see tangled with the foam
The smiling body battered by the shore,
And his lone heart home.

'Ever why, O ever, ever why?'
Besought his angel and the lovely moon
Her tragic follower; and both reply:

'You are the tragedy, the human mirth,
'The lunar holocaust torn by the tides
'Of sneering lips, and little laughing eyes,
'Strange one, god-bound, destined from the earth
'By commendation to a sea-god's arms,
'The night your mother laboured in your birth,
'She groaned out charms,
'Bidding all winds harbour in her hair
'And all the seas lave coolness on her brow
'And snatch you there.
'Wild ringing was the plea, and hearing this,
'Saturn shook the night with one great laugh –
'And made you his.'[38]

63

Toni's

Look! There is beauty lying here!
In the dimness of the lane
It flashes as it would declare
All the twilight air
To be a foil for its gay light –
Oranges little suns,
Lemon moons and pears that once
Blushed red at Melba's sight,
Heaped and tumbled up like lamps
Along a river,
While the vendor stamps
His feet that shiver
As he waits,
Sniffing at the orchard tones
He uses for his bait
To lure the crowds. The whole lane owns
Italian flavour, mottled joy
And often, someone passing sees
The sparkling stall, breathes scents that tease,
And swears it is Hesperides!

Sonnet: après Baudelaire

I am torn between my soul and you,
The wanting and the will at variance.
Yielding to green eyes where shadows dance
Would be an easy thing if chance once drew
Warm hand to hand. The quick days glance
By torturing the flesh, yet flesh entrance.
My dear, this hour must know, so let me view

Your bright hair, twist and turn again your head
And so complete this fight of soul and sense.
The days are dying. Soon shall we be dead
To all save wonders that this hour must hear
O shall I? God! My proffered hand grows tense,
For I am strangely frightened with you near.[39]

Sonnet [2]

This love has more of spirit than of flesh,
For we have met on peaks of imagery
Watching clouds whorl upwards from the sea
To tangle all the blue within their mesh.
See how the beating winds that coldly thresh
The wool against the air, snatch fiercely
Our hearts from matter's clue, as if there be
More loving in the soul when form is ash.

    And we shall go on meeting where the heights
    Of unmade dreams mount upwards to the moon.
    Follow dear. My hands are full of lights
    Star-drawn. Bend your head. This is the hour
    When mind with heart may move; for very soon
    All the flesh will wither like a flower.[40]

To Laurie [2]

Charmed like a moon-slaked orchard, here the streets
Laurel-lined, catch silver from the lamps –
Fire gifts. Watch the star-light, lamp-light stamp
The sneaking shadows back. A dark lane beats
Its windy doors protestingly, and meets
The offered light with dark, while knocking vamps
Strange basses to the blindman's buff that ramps
A sullen gratitude, thanks incomplete.

       Not thus I spurn the light within your hand.
       But more than light, blue in jewelled fire
       Moon-harvests all my mind. O softly, friend,
       Stranger, pulling like an urgent river
       Comes gratitude, heart-deep in poor attire –
       Far more than all the gifts – there is the giver.

And again

How awkward just to offer thanks
Not for the gift so much, as giver.
Trite words come in sounding ranks.
How awkward just to offer thanks
That gently break the mundane banks
To say one word that leaves a quiver –
How awkward just to offer thanks –
Not for the gift so much, as giver.

To a Poet

The little minutes run me home
To the fireside of your words,
Racing by me, brown-winged foam
Of an autumn flight of birds.
This hill, and then the street –
No limbs so fleet.

Gently I move back the door,
Shadows shift along the wall.
O my warmth and heart's red core
Seated there! The ashes fall
Soft, white. And as I bend –
The soul's bright end.

Clown

To everybody with due exceptions
You were the japer
Black-tasselled fooler,
Hearts cut from paper
And pinned to your sleeve,
Black and white mocker,
Laughter was quick on the lips
Seeing your worth,
Emaciate under
The passing of days and the ebbing of wonder.
Primary loving saw nothing of laughing
I was believer –
So lend me your gown
I held a creed born of deceiver,
I was the clown.

She

Grief is thin as the moon.
O the dark hair weeping
Down on the arms and neck
And the sad flesh sleeping.

Cover the crescent.
A fire still warm and red
Streaks the massed woods behind,
And the gipsy's head;

Strikes on two copper bangles,
Her cheek. And here
The river adds tears to her dreams –
O my dear! O my dear!

Sonnet [3]

This might be finality, the aim
Of all I ever hoped to have – not end,
Perhaps – but where, in course of time, ascend
Love-wishes of a life, to find their claim
Realised in the one. That I might frame
My life to yours, and wayward wantings bend
Into submission, so I choose; and tend
My thoughts to this as children in a game.

Still, should this die and leave for noonday years
Another lover with a brighter smile
Who'd gather as a reaper does the ears
Of corn grown yellow in a summer season,
I would resist his arm and blade, the while
My heart still cried for you – and sought the reason.[41]

Sonnet [4]

Silently let's pause beside the dawn
Where the round hills are blinking back the dark,
Their heads wind-towsled, and as softly, mark
The frost grey gullies steaming forth a yawn
Of misty silver. Strategic as a pawn
Among the patchwork fields, a wee house stark
By the crimson east has panes ablaze, an arc
Sun-circled gilds the sleepy trees, night-charcoal-drawn.

     Now you can be content, for we have seen
     The sun's death at the birth of yellow moons
     Attended by a million stars and been
     Into the white noon, hung in drowsy dusk
     Like two great moths. And we'll have known soon
     The first ray stab the hills with flaming tusk.

Edward Street

The uphill street and casual tram,
Gaunt buildings in the afternoon
Press receptive traces on the brain,
Reminding, thrusting in the day-time dream
Of you and your green hills.
I wonder, perplexedly imaging
You, lapped upon a noon-tide on a hill-slope
Country-roads resounding to your foot-steps,
And the long dark lazy after-dinner doze.
There is no ending
To the up-hill street with its sadness
No finish to the down-hill fields of greenness,
Nor to the aching in my hands, my hands
Longing incessantly [for] your own
Their comforting touch.[42]

Culture, 1945

'It's symbolistic, dear, that's what it is!
'You'd never guess at first, I know. But see,
'It's merely self-expression. What? My dear,
'Of course there's no repression these days. Art
'Is what the artist cares to give us. Look –
'That eye behind the swan's wing on the right
'Is meant to represent a breadth of vision
'Such as all these great Bohemians have …
'You wonder that the artist called it "Life"?
'Then note the hand that clasps a little dust
'(Of bone no doubt). It's clear that you must read;
'We've Freud and Nietzsche at our finger-tips,
'And all that sort of thing. O darling, stop
'Gaping at that Holbein; here's the finest –
'And that ghastly "Sunset on a Hill" –
'Picasso right behind you, and Matisse,
'Must you dear? – da Vinci makes me ill!'[43]

Translations from French

Astley's French studies at The University of Queensland were an important influence on her poetry. The following poems are examples of her translations from French lyric poets made in 1945 and 1946.

Ballad (translated from Hugo)

If you like, let's make a dream
And fleeing if we could
Upon two palfreys, captives seem
A bird sings in the wood.

Luggage is necessity
We'll carry vows and prayer,
Our fortunes and our misery,
And the flower of your hair.

We shall enter at the inn
And we shall pay the host
With your smile that lacks all sin,
With my scholar's toast.

You the Lady, I the lord!
Come, my heart is bright,
Dear, we'll tell it word for word
To the stars at night.[44]

Chinary

It is not you, fair lady, whom I love,
No longer you, nor you my Juliet,
Ophelia, nor Beatrice; nor golden
Laura's large sweet eyes with vows beset.

The maiden whom I love now, has her bower
In China, by the Yellow River's tide
And dwells with her aged parents in a tower
Of porcelain; with cormorants beside.

She has her eyes upturned; a foot so small
It fits within the hand; and to this weds
Skin clearer than the brass of lamps; and all
Her nails are long and deeply flushed with red.

Her head the swallow brushes with his wings,
She sways before the lattice in her room;
And every night, like any poet sings
Of the willow, and the peach-tree's bloom.[45]

The sadly sobbing strings
Of weeping violins
In autumn days
Scar my timid heart
With a langorous art
And dewey haze.

Choking fast for breath
And pallid quite as death
When chimes the hour
Through the flowing tears
I summon my lost years
Time would devour.

And sorrowing I go –
Heart, head-heavy so
On a wind of grief
Which bears me here and there
Tortured in my care
Like a dead leaf.[46]

1946

In 1946 Astley failed history and economics subjects at The University of Queensland because she was typing an Honours dental thesis for a man she 'fell in love' with.[47] Apart from translations from French poets, mainly Alfred de Musset, her poetry production also seems to have declined during this year, when she was supporting her university studies by teaching for two days a week at Lourdes Hill College in Brisbane.

Rain after Drought

Three days behind full moon,
Passing our pain,
With wind in the arms of the north
Comes ripple of rain.

Only the smoke lay low
Where the fields were wet.
Houses smiled – and our hearts –
And the dark sun set.

Surely the eyes smile often
Through their pain.
'What pain in love,' you ask, 'when love should soften
'Loss to gain,
'Make one day memory-rich?'
To which
I say that love was born in weeping
As we – who first know grief while mirth comes after
Even through tears
We learn the way to laughter.[48]

The flesh can bear a hurt, eradicate
With all the ease of night eclipsing sun
Its human wounds. But let a sorrow run
Into the heart's green fields, let swords debate
In steel about a soul once consecrate
To happiness, the scar remains; and done
Is joy. See how the pliant brain would shun
Hurt that time can not eliminate.

      Yes, stab the soul, and then its urgent mind
      Takes in a pain, grief-fraught, and clipped with wonder,
      O the aching never ceases! Cold, we find
      That memories have many limbs to spread
      Terror-tendrils. – Love once quoted dead,
      Lives, though the pirate years swarm in for plunder.[49]

Juvenilia

All we regret, we singers in the sun,
Is the long age coming after, wasted days,
Senility of withered mind. No ways
Lead to avoidance save the mortal one,
And we have no thought of death, and death is done
With, but for that regret, the sixties' haze
Of gravery and gossip, harmless teas, and praise –
Fruit bitter for the fact youth gave no name.

       We are afraid of age, not for its lack
       Of physical advantage, like a flower
       Wrinkled and sapless; not that we must track
       Into a place of pain, but just because
       We may forget ideals, as in an hour,
       Even the rose forgets what once it was.[50]

Adulthood

Astley began Exercise Book B, the later of the school exercise books that together contain most of her poetry, as a publishable collection, but did not complete her project.[51] She wrote 'Thea Gregson' on the front cover, and 'Rejects mostly' in the space provided for 'Grade'. In contrast with the poems in A, most of B's poems seem never to have been published, and no correspondence relating to their publication survives in Astley's Fryer Library archive.

Inside B's cover Astley wrote the planned volume's dedication, 'For John', meaning her husband, Jack Gregson. Thea and Jack married at the Gympie courthouse north of Brisbane on 27 August 1948. Most of the poems in Exercise Book B postdate their wedding, which, because Jack was a Protestant and a divorcé, caused a break between Astley and her parents that lasted until the birth of her son Edmund in 1955.[52] The young couple moved to Sydney in January 1949. The poems that Astley gathered for her unpublished collection therefore span what was probably her most important life transition.

Poems early in B are handwritten; most of the later poems are typed and pasted in. Although she included in her collection poems written between 1945 and 1948 – some of which relate to her courtship and wedding – Astley wrote most of the poems that she assembled in B while working as a high school teacher in Sydney between 1949 and 1957. In her 1986 interview with Jennifer Ellison, she stated that she wrote her first novel, *Girl with a monkey* (which was commended in 1956 in a literary competition in *The Sydney Morning Herald*) 'about 1955', *i.e.* when she was nearly thirty. After Angus and Robertson published *Girl with a monkey* in 1958, prose fiction became Astley's preferred genre. She nevertheless transferred many of the skills that she had learned as a poet into her fiction, and many themes persist across the change in genres.

In contrast with the poems in Section I, most of the poems that follow in Section II are the work of an experienced poet who has developed her unique style through study, trial and effort sustained from childhood. The poems in Section II are printed with Astley's titles (or are untitled) and follow the order of dates that she assigned to them. Poems handwritten into B seem to have been composed in 1950 or earlier. The poems that Astley typed and pasted into the middle pages of B contain no dates, but their known dates of publication suggest that they are later than 1950. '8/6/57' is written in Astley's hand on the inside of B's back cover.

Section II as far as and including 'The Purist' (135) contains all the poems that Astley chose for her collection, but reorders them according to dates of writing and/or publication, as far as these are known.

Astley's unpublished collection

Let me plant a tune or buy a singing bird
To make your dusk a lovelier affair.
I'd rather plant a tune – there's more delight
In wondering the colour of the themes.
Nebulous, and yet as real as if
A hundred little boughs should burst in song
Shaking all their life out to be heard.
But then, I think I'd rather buy a singing bird
So that each star might hear it every night
That creeps like dust across the moon-soaked town,
Bending and curving over garden rail
Waiting for the rainfall of its song,
While the river reaches mute from grey to brown
And then to black and black …
Let me buy the bird and plant the tune,
Do both. And then I'll know you tangibly
In all this vapoured life.
Up with the moon![53]

To reconcile four seasons in a day!
(Dreamer's endeavour!)
Carelessly sever
All a slow year's plans, heap, reap away
Time – barriers to bonfires of the will?
Yes, would, and still.

You laughed – and summer gleamed and held me so
Warm with your laughter,
No wonder, after,
I found your arm had seen a winter's snow
An autumn in your eyes, and startled! – there
Soft springtime hair![54]

Ashgrove Hills

O the gentleness on my soul
Is not of your making.
But a soft winter's day takes swift toll
Of my love, and its aching.
I would wish to be certain and hold with no doubt
That under this feeling
The pang and the throb have died out
With no harsh appealing.

But I know on my entering back
To the street and its houses
Yourself will come swift on my track
Awaking and making the lack
This old passion arouses,
Teasing the wound in my soul,
Stabbing and taking swift toll.
O the street and the houses![55]

Letter to Nathalie

This brain once rich
With new translations of old things
Huddles mere ashes.
Those wonders which
I would for you – long summerings –
Are haven-spent.
The heart was withered in a sophist's spring
When blood flowed red,
Generous into an impulse given head
And reckless lent.
And even when the heart enquired of spring
The heart was dead.

This brain once lavish
With words responsive to an hour
Reflects no scene.
Hears only rain song.
Dear, would weep, but only sees in flower
At morning, everywhere,
This sudden green.[56]

Flesh-fettered so I plead to clasp the real
Some living tangibility to know
At last a quiet fulfilment ere I go
Hearing the years' bronze tongues clang peal on peal
Dirge for a dreamer – even past griefs feel
Incompleteness, even past loves show
Like broken Venuses – where words would flow
A void, and where emotions, there a weal.

Music was found wanting, and long after
I thought a summer's day was made my own
Love killed the scene, then love dissolved in laughter,
Moments of sea and bush half-felt, half-known,
Those gropings after loveliness! I stand
Fettered in flesh and dust within my hand.[57]

Echo Point

I shall remember though the years deny
All cognisance of time and thought and mood:

This is a place of great valleys sweeping
Down to green sunlight and blue peaks
Piercing the cold winds from the west.

Though years mount up black-towered fright
I shall remember my throat longing towards music
And my fingers urged to the flowers that grew sudden along
    the path.[58]

Tomorrow

Today's intensity lies dying
With darkness balming the mind
Comes relaxation of the soul,
Passions put by wearily
Into dingy corners for tomorrow.
I am aware part-touching time,
Of unexpected glories in the morn
Flushed with an element of wonder,
And know my motley
For hoping thus some gold beatitude
Of days unknown, when sure I know
The roads will still wind brightly
As today, cruel ribbons into sunlight,
As today, trees bear green benison
As today, and hours move empty,
And a lovelessness, and the little town.[59]

John

All night during the wind
to the undertones of door and shutter swung
below in an empty house,
I gather the darkness around me
forgetting your face.

And though I would remember
only this or this – but never you – the dark
blooms with a savagery of flowers
all memory-quick – and I
am remembering your mouth.

Down corridors woven with wind
all night long, my hand is stretched to pluck
flowers curved away at my touch.
I cry out your name and hear only
the shutters swing back, and back.[60]

Hunters Hill [1]

These quiet houses, river-lost, tremble away
Under plane tree or sky.
I laugh, or sing, or feel my blood
Trembling away too – and I cry.

Perhaps these winter preludes touch old wandering griefs
At the thought of doors
Shuddered against the bitter sunsets,
And my feet, time-tortured, crave
Familiar floors.[61]

Hunters Hill [2]

No trees are witnesses, or she
Caught in a green crowd
Might feel a new terror
Pluck at her shroud.

Listless-lying under the wet earth
Slow moisture cries
Into the hopeless skull
For the bone's surprise.

No trees are witnesses, or she
Feeling their touch
Might think death incomplete –
And wonder much.[62]

I must be cursed by some black doom
That took from me the Midas touch
Of finding laughter in the sun –
I don't mind much.

Or should the stars long pulverized
By tyrant moons, motes in the air
Swing their black curtains past my eyes –
I couldn't care!

I might have minded once
But years on years
Of pain like this have dried
My blood of tears.

By paradox, more bonds
The more I'm free.
Dear, what a fool you are
To fool with me![63]

Over the young backyards each day, and I
Older with each new sun, to work
In the trembling mornings;
To gaze unbelieving at the smug tiled roofs,
The washing freshly hung, and faces
Devoid of cunning in the hour-old light.
We are all moving, Mr. Jacoby
And the Polish Jew Szperi moving
Pimply young puffed up air-raid-proved
Macarthy working on night-shift,
Moving.
When you see this flattened landscape
Creeping like a tired crustacean
Over a sea-bed; when you see
Tired claws of suburbs scrabbling
At the greenness, pray for us now.
Be St. Jerome, be Crysostom, O doctores
Be Loyola ecstatic in battle.
But do not be Edward Gregory Johnson
Clerk, eight fifty, family of five
Secure within your tank of fibrolite
Manned with umbrellas![64]

Sonnet [5]

Sometimes, incredibly, the longing swings
Into the quiet rivers of my blood,
For the old places, the time-lost evenings
Sharp with friends' voices. God! What creatures bud

Out of a sudden whim to flaunt before
My pain laid bare, flesh-petalling away
Till I am only pain, and must explore
Again this love or that, familiar fray

On still-remembered carpets, harsh tongues tasting
My foibles, moon-bright roads and headlamps flinging
The crouching country back, and O the waiting
Of café conversations, and the singing –

      Above all else that singing! I remember
      A girl's young voice one breathless hot December.[65]

Magnetic

Thoughts pointed to the pole-star of the mind
Move in to light from outer dark like ships
Unhurried. O what captained words these lips
May now loose from their harbourage to find
The self's bright centre, timorous, inclined
Before my own heart's tempest. Moonlight strips
Shadow from sail and sail moon-painted dips,
Tacking towards that centre foam defined.

  Reached up with tenderness the rocky arms
  Lave water down the sideways leaning sky
  Cloud-curdled and star-moist. Upon my brow
  Winds patterned with palmetto find the calms
  Beyond great longing. Young I magnify
  The island moving in across the prow.[66]

Sonnet [6]

The thin lights of each day's disguise recede.
Back from the mouth, the brow, the eyes, the hands,
These masks sophisticate are loosed indeed;
From lovely terraces of flesh the bands

Slip quietly to bare the fearful soul,
And bough on bough the startled thoughts take flight
In images that scatter and unroll
Darknesses of truth become too bright.

So I each day, beyond the working hours,
Break through the veil that keeps me from the air
To taste exquisitely the scent of flowers,
Or feel the wind carve pictures with my hair.

      Such understanding holds such pain it must
      Reduce mouth, brow, eyes, hands to living dust.

Satori

Taking the day as primal postulate,
Using this berried hedge for argument,
(And with what logic does the slow descent
Of this brown hill move into blue debate
With hill on hill!) I find the truth inflate
Almost beyond belief the ripe intent
Of premises of pollen drowned in scent.
I must conclude a godhead, integrate

> Myself with some keen wisdom where God's laughter
> Lies like trellised leaves across the summer
> Apricot-coloured sky. You were not wrong,
> Knowing the mercy that would follow after,
> To press me to this pilgrimage – newcomer,
> Half-deafened by these thunderstorms of song.

Neap

You may be sure I know my neap
Washes you in antipodal tides,
Drawn by moons as gold as grins
Of amusement parks on harbour-sides

Where sailors flutter bifurcate
Along the windy asphalt quays
To bluster with the blowsy girls
Below the city's building frieze.

This plum-blue air of nine o'clock
So harshly ripe with seeds of light,
Becomes in Capricornian terms
Day tropical, so blinding bright

You may not know that at the ebb
Thus islanded upon your sea,
Within the body's unsolved woods
One bird keeps singing desperately.

Had wished because of Celtic fears
Like drunkenness in a gipsy's mind
Never to think of loving you
In case the thought that I designed

Should stop your love. Dearest, had wished
As yellow trees must ache for spring,
Never to think of having you
Lest flight-forced by imagining.

But never to think, O never have –
Too much for the flesh and heart of me!
I'll dream – and should my fears prove true,
What bitter-sweet annullity!

No more need these lips song-sue
Sky, nor young bones feel unfed
With half-complete sensation;
No more these fingers try green leaves
For sap, or hue
With eyes, and know instead
Of pain-shot joy, a tired imitation.
I came to the shelter of your eaves.

And no more need this flesh awarely
Tapping for beauty in the dark
All agonizing quiver
Like moth new-moist beneath the sun
But find where sheerly
Passions rise to a stark
Monument of minutes for the lover,
And bend all truths into this strange new one.

You know now. I've not said.
What can be said
When moon-daubed streets and stars displace
All sense and careful wisdom from my head? –
Turn me your face.

My eyes bright? I've not smiled.
How could have smiled
When warmth of tears would overflow
To see you turn. Remember, love's a child –
You must not go.[67]

Futility appears the total day,
The useless consummation. Interest
Comes with irrelevance. And laughter pressed
From adult lips, is hollow with decay
As if it never were amused, nor may
Be at the puppet race's paltry jests
Which drift, unsavoury scum upon the breast
Of too transparent waters lapped on clay.

      O children are the warm and lovely things,
      And while they're young and also very wise.
      Before maturity grows close and clings
      With parasitic cares and sophistries,
      Their laughter is the warming of my soul,
      The culminating joy, the end, the whole.

Those were the months we found the summer texture
Too personal to bear, too ripely full
Of dust, too prickling on the skin;
Or moving through the ergot grass
Garbing the cape, the horses
Blossoming with sweat along the saddle-line.
Remember then the kiosks
Crowded with summer folks and yelling boys
Half under hoofs and trampled
By their own curiosity; the trial
Run on hard sand with salt
Driving the horses crazy and our hearts
Pounding together.

I beg you, all might soon dissolve, but this,
This must impregnate our night with soul.
Tired I am of twilight love, a kiss
Scattered like a petal, part for whole.

Yesterday I groaned beneath the sun
Poised on metaphysical beliefs
Of living's estimate, and wanted done
To death the flesh, but most of all heart's griefs

And bastard tears. And now you harrow hurt
With half-said things, a Plautine comedy
Where laughter is an anguish. Dear, desert
Those falterings which keep you back from me.

     There is no love but us, and what love spares
     Niggardly from the hungry tiger years.[68]

Sulpicia Ill

Half of my kith and less of my kin
Have long passed me over,
Pursuing no plan but to counteract sin
Of lover with lover.

I ask me why years should beacon like this
In diminishing torches
Long galleries of loving that point to a kiss
And some passionate matches.

Of laughter perhaps. But the truth is it matters
Far less than the pleading
That thread sighs to thread when the day's fabric tatters
While half the heart's bleeding.[69]

You of the heart and I
And the midnight roads
Wanderers of them find analogy
In the heart's dark windings:
Streets beating back the quickened emphasis
Of feet on the pavement,
(Dreamy gulfs of doorways),
Hand hard, warm around my own,
And then the sudden impulse to look up,
Look down. O the volubility
Of our smiling eyes.

Fragment

Through the translucency of rain
The topmost conifers
Swing in giant arcs to invisible wind.
Only driving across small yards the pattern
Changes from perpendicular to swathed
Arcs of grey string, to scarves
Of water coiled about buildings.
Even without this visibility
I could divine through iron roofing
Drumming monotones of weather,
These switching geometries of rain and wind.

Lament

Last week the lugger's in
All blistering from the coral waterways
With the sail licking and the fawning wind.
So sails for eight days now have lain tired,
Masts somehow thin.

We girls should comb our hair
Like long seas running hyacinthine blue
To capture men and cargoes. Here's my fear –
Lost between voyages in my own port,
No lover where? …

Summer

Within the cage of bones the sullen
Lion that is I paces the parquetry
Of days, yawning stalely
Into the spring. Buds and tendrils
Reflect on convex windows'
Deepest blue, but the tawny gold
Hair-tossing watcher
Sees the geometry of wings indifferent,
The convolutions of the vine
Unmoved, and threatens only
To leap into the grasslands lying
Like green water along the littoral.
Dive, drown, dissolve in fathoms
Of thin blades – buffalo, bamboo, festuca.

A Warning

So I said smiling quietly: See
The summer air is striped with rain,
And all your soft-leafed errant loves
Climb on the trellis of my pain.

And though you've husked the juices out
From some five souls before my coming,
How long can your bright leaves withstand
This rain's incessant drumming?

Dunes

Some spikenard
Of yellow flowers, last year's remembered. Twisting
Across the multiplicity of purple
Bloom on the land-side,
Swings all remembrance down the rhyming beaches
Bitten by sea, by wind.

So would I lie
All through late summer cushioned on their hard roundness,
Sifting the coloured dust through sunburnt fingers,
Watching a sand-tide
Dam up the spiny grass in golden reaches
While the slow surf dinned.

Or half-asleep
On these dry snows, lips lazily compressing
A fruit's last sticky juices, melt in laughter
On flinging my hand wide
To hear companionate the blue sea stretches
Sucking the shore's white rind.[70]

Last Week

'Hand me your hat and I will pour
'All Thursday in like clear creek water,
'From the moment the sun burst through the door,
'Until the white moon splintered the shutter.'

'Shall you drink or I, and would it mean
'We have trapped in flesh the multiple sweetness
'That morning gave and the brumous green
'Of fig trees wearing the evening lateness?'

'You may only look to discover our faces
'Drowned in those minutes. I would not swim
'If I could from those tender Thursday places
'To grope for Friday around the brim.'

Picnic

Clean on the valley's edge of afternoon,
Five of us, conversational-wise above
The far-down creek — so far we swim in air —
Pursue our words through patterned brother-love.

This is a day for birds to cut with arcs
Wind-shifting geometry in upper sky,
Tangent upon a dried-out shell of moon
Unsolved at four o'clock by wing or eye.

Our words construct a geometry as well.
More lovely than these birds the problems rise
Planing against the mind's grey sullen hills;
Word-bright our theorems tease each other's eyes.

Poem [6]

You are my quiet music, you
My house roof under rain
And my door opening or window
Light letting in, light out.
Ever dear, you are those little paths
Winding in to one veracity
Like sudden glimpses of a sea
So loved it breaks the heart,
So ultimate, the journey meant
Nothing in pain.
Those sudden lamp-pools touching back
Fears and the dark, are you;
These books, these fires in the evening
Warmth eating into the heart
Through dazzled eyes sleep-closing
Till you are sleep, sleep, and somehow – thresholds.[71]

Solvency

In acres and oceans bright green on blue wave bending
Windways to pattern eyes with sudden light
Shaken from shore-line palms on sand-gold lending
Motes of wild summer brilliance to my sight,

How richly have I plundered place and season
Acalyphas twin-bursting into fruit
And tamarinds whose scent compels the reason
To see the splitting rinds as so much loot

Garnered by solstice in the summer rising.
This. And the mango trees all pointilliste
With yellow bulbs red-stippled for my prizing.
I cannot believe that in this I play priest;

Make sacrifice and watch the white smoke spread
Such cumulus of wealth above my head.

Love in Our Time

Always and reasonably, it is sad
That one should so impersonalize
Question and answer in the flesh,
Reducing to a brief schedule
Form-to-be-filled-relationship
Woman with man.

The woman questing in the truth
Acts out the essence of a lie
To please the partner who must see
Himself more willing than she wills,
While both behind their guarded eyes
Know truth for lies.

I'll lean along the driving rain
To watch the stippling of the river
Lie lonely beneath hull or bridge
Or plantain penniform; discover

The textured substance dimpled with
Pellets of cloud which sculpture water
Strangely with self. These early trades
Stripe air and buildings, all that matter.

Invocation

For Frederick Delius

Play Hansel to my Gretel in this forest
Of plunging, tossing sound.
Phrases like tree-vines caught
Under the wind of trumpets, hurled across
Sky-mind, patterning with point
Curling sorites of the brain and ear.
Some bird-like clarinet might dart
Across the massy greens of ringing leaves
And chase a smaller flute into the blue.

O logic, that we chase, is lost and drowns
Under the flying storm amid the leaves,
The ballet impulse of the summer trees.

Choose that great tender fig where we might die
Battered by flying chords.
These solemn woods press so invisibly
The singing flesh, the eyes must darken.[72]

Droving Man

She might have chosen cities, but the man
Compelled to see the pastures of his soul
Stocked with dream-cattle
Turned north and west and sunwards to his goal
Under the freckled lightning of the wattle.

Over the years the piccaninny thoughts
And timid lubra words became so shy
Of their own thunder,
They never spoke together but his eye
Would find in hers a startled twin of wonder.[73]

Lubra

The girl stood where the wind
made flowers of her hair,
feeling its tides rescind
year from year.

Summer drooped and spring
on her mouth grew red.
She held, as listening,
her delicate head.

Cool on the flesh it sang
till the soul lay bare,
where bell-towers clashed and rang –
and their ropes were hair!

And she as a tree was bent,
but the wind moved on,
the hair-flowers faded, rent.
The girl was gone.

Whitsunday

This is true Pentecost, this downward heat
Of sun in sharp angle, sun on reef waters. Why,
The broad illumination of the sky
Curved brightness, fire and sea reflection meet
In fine furious fathoms of air and beat
The yellow beach like brass deep-dented, dry
With divers tongues of fescue grass that cry
Sand-hill gospels for beach-combers' feet.

      No Pentecostal dove, but here a gull
      Above the passage islands coastwards tunes
      Along the trade wind following the hull
      Of some fish-hungry craft to where blue bay
      Dozes between the paws of sleepy dunes –
      The tired silver lions of Whitsunday.

Descant

For three nights now we two have lain
Under rain-stippled roof and heard
These points of silence barricade the house,
The room, the whispered word.

O should my hand seek out the warm
Intelligence of loving limb,
Ten desperate messengers of flesh
Interpret silently my whim

And barricade your loneliness
Within my own – and both aware
Exquisitely of house and room
And whispered word and rain-striped air.[74]

A Last Year's Hero

You wore autumnally the wreathier wreath,
Gargantuan, laureate, obsessed with bravery,
And who apart from me beneath that bold
Too candid stare perceived the knavery?

Spread-eagled curule-fashion, powerful cars,
Profile Roman-minted, public-wise;
Yet I bore fasces in those early months,
And kept my axe-blade blunt, and my replies.

But somewhere in those laurel avenues
Too thickly branched, too leafed with adulation
You struck a merchant's bargain with your heart
Turned politic to reap the situation

Down to the last denarius, the last
Plaudit self-tuned to multiply your gain.
And who apart from me in all that smiling
Crowd of flatterers received such pain?[75]

A Seasonal Lament

Here boredom works through plangency
Of drumming monotones of weather
And all the grief of sky and tree
And room and self are merged together

Under this ringing roof of iron
Surely some palliative must
Light up the eyes that track the clock
Through minutes settling down like dust.

O I should lay my head within
The thinner comfort of my arm
And focus through these sleepy lids
The hachured sky beyond the palm.

The Purist

The totals of his thought were colourless
Perfect in their two-dimensional form
Tricked out in black on white, the pedant's norm
Of utterance. Yet roused he could express
Only within the limits of his dress
World agonies, class struggle, personal storm
Without a warm man's sometime need for warm
Phrase or barbarous oath or jargoned stress.

> The restlessness of language like a sea
> Will split the raft infinitives apart
> And drown each cliché, each fatuity
> Of careful speech under the tides' blue-bright
> Uncluttered sweeps' parabolas that start
> From shore of sense vernacularly right.[76]

Occasional poems

While Thea Astley was compiling her collection for Exercise Book B, she composed a few further poems that responded to changing circumstances. One such circumstance was her employment from 1967 as a tutor in English at Macquarie University, where she came into contact with fellow poet J M Couper.

Short Story

All through the month of August
The ship lay like a leaf,
Lightly between the mangroves
And the reef.

So moon-drunk in the evenings,
Reaping the bearded shore,
Swayed moon-drunk the sailor
To my door;

And every morning promised
To stand off with the tide.
But still the moon grew sick
And thinly died.

The blistered boat moved little
Under the clear white sun,
And she and we lay lightly
For thirty days and one.[77]

On hearing the first cuckold in spring

Those plagal cadences lamenting
Your meagre loss are selfish sir!
You'll find next season him assenting
In plagal cadences lamenting
Equinoctial pranks, repenting
Birds, buds, bees, but mainly her.
Those plagal cadences lamenting
Your meagre loss are selfish sir![78]

Horace 1. v

Pyrrha, who's the slender fellow
Now, scent-daubed, drowning in roses
Courts you in soft summer houses?
For whom do you lie back that yellow

Dense simplicity of hair?
How often he'll lament the fickle
Gods, your honour; naïf, puzzle
Calm seas grown sharp in darkening air.

Who now, too trusting, reaps that bloom;
Landlubber, ignorant of the sea,
Expects you always tender, free?
Unhappy wretches, those for whom

Untried, you glitter! As for me
A votive plaque on temple wall
To powerful sea god tells it all –
And clothes still dripping from the sea![79]

Written in reply to J.M. Couper's 'Abelard to Eloise'

Only monkish cant could turn
(forgive me, tutor) that first premise
love in Christ without the flesh,
the Church plague-argument: to burn
is better than to marry – see it? –
into its converse half and make
anatomy the total as you grieve it.

Too many bodies endlessly
pour into bodies – here's the laugh! –
while *mind* keeps itching wordlessly.
Believe me, you've kept the better half.[80]

Landfall at night; the long seas took me in.
Touched beach and would have drowned but for the sense
Of voyaging now over, other self
Discovered. Found at morning an immense

Landscape of sudden green and unknown trees
So tall the heart cried home, surprised from pain
Of desert days by pasture now so thick
It might have taken life to cross this plain

And reach those troubled peaks sawing at blue.
Feet move. The journey starts. But as days pass
Face mirrors feet's disbelief. Who would have guessed
At such deep quicksand underneath such grass?[81]

After Tasman

Charted your coast without once touching land
Spinning on shore tides. Land would have me drowned
Earth-drenched, the weed tangled, hills in waves
Mounting until the seventh seized me. Found

Sea to be safer, sea between the islands
Running white with gulls, gull-lonely, green –
Sea-scaped along your earth, whilst I saw
Guessed at, rather, dune-hidden, still unseen

The inland gentleness beyond the peaks
Scaled at first assault the tender miles
Grass-warm with summer and my thin white feet
Exploratory and tentative as smiles.

EDITOR'S AFTERWORD

I wrote poetry when I was younger. Most writers cut their teeth on it. I think if you've written poetry you're better adjusted to finding suitable rhythms in prose.[82]

Poetry in the adolescent years, which is like a form of acne – 'I think I'm having a poem'.[83]

These excerpts demonstrate Thea Astley's undecided attitudes later in life to the poetry to which she devoted her creative energies as a teenager and young woman. Ambivalence is evident too in the scattered and incomplete forms in which she passed on her poetic legacy. Astley's poems survive as handwritten or typed and pasted-in pages in school exercise books, as loose leaves in Fryer Library folders, as marginalia in her university copy of *The Oxford book of French verse*, and as occasional pieces in newspapers, anthologies and magazines. The 1930s and 1940s magazines in which

Astley most consistently published her poems – *All Hallows' magazine*, *Barjai: a meeting place for youth*, and The University of Queensland student journal *Galmahra* – survive mostly as rare copies in libraries. The present edition has therefore been a search-and-rescue mission, and some decisions about selecting and ordering poems have been finely balanced.

The 116 selected poems make up about half of Astley's known poetic output. The criteria applied have been, in order: merit; relevance to Astley's development as a poet and fiction writer; and completeness, *i.e.* whether a particular poem survives in a form that Astley seems to have regarded as final. Her manuscript ticks against poems are sometimes a clue to the third criterion.

In deciding the order of printing, I have been guided primarily by Astley's year headings, her dating of individual poems and by dates of publication where these are known. Ordering according to date is an obvious choice in respect of her earlier exercise book (A), which is a sequential bundling of her school and university poems. However, Astley began her later exercise book (B) as a publishable collection, and her intention, which ought to be acknowledged, cuts across what might otherwise have been a simple date-based ordering of poems throughout the entire selection.

Accordingly, in Section II I have commemorated her plan by printing poems that she considered worthy of anthologising under the heading 'Astley's unpublished collection', but reordered them by date. This decision was made firstly because we cannot know at what point in B Astley lost interest in publishing her collection, and secondly because date ordering reveals her developing skills as a poet in relation to her biography.

Astley's school poems are romantic effusions influenced by Wordsworth's and Hopkins' nature mysticism. By contrast, the poems that she wrote between 1943 and 1946, while she was a university student, trainee teacher and member of the *Barjai* group, focus on verbal techniques and experiment with a range of forms, principally the sonnet. Her main models at this point were Shakespeare and the French and Latin lyrists. The present selection represents the twenty-four translations in Astley's Fryer archive by six poems that testify to her fascination with imagery and with the patterns and sounds of words. Although Astley gradually learned to moderate this fascination in her prose fiction, it persisted to the end of her writing life. In her last novel, *Drylands*, published in 1999, she used alliteration and metaphor to reiterate the point:

A word could have a whole fiction buried within. One word, monosyllabic or polysyllabic – take your pick – opened up a worldscape of ideas that could laze in bliss under summer soothings or become a maelstrom of conflict.[84]

The largest group of poems that Astley wrote between leaving school in 1942 and marrying Jack Gregson in 1948 are lyrics that address themes of love, friendship, loneliness, rejection, submission, joy, conflict, pain and despair. Some of these add urgency and dread to poetry's traditional obsession with the passing of time. Yet other poems deal less personally with poets, music, myths and legends, or take the form of made-up or extrapolated scenarios. Examples of the latter are 'From Troy' (22), 'The Card Players' (57) and 'Roland to Arlène' (58). By contrast, poems such as 'Grey Afternoon' (29), 'To My Brother' (52), 'The Sailor' (61), 'Toni's' (64), 'Edward Street' (74) and 'Ashgrove Hills' (94) are solidly grounded in wartime and immediately post-war Brisbane and Melbourne. These poems of Astley's university and teacher-training years temporarily suspend her high-school preoccupation with nature. However, Queensland's outdoors – its beaches, islands and seascapes, rainforests, Brisbane's bayside, the Gold and Sunshine Coasts and their hinterlands, the dry and wet tropics, and burnt-out interior – later resurfaced as an important repository of meaning across her entire prose *oeuvre*. Finally, 'Culture, 1945' (75), which enunciates conservative views on the visual arts and on public sexual expression, initiates what was to shape itself in Astley's fiction into a strand of satire and irony.

Astley sometimes keys the poems in B, which are among her best, to her travels or changes of residence in the late 1940s and the 1950s, when she visited or taught in inner Brisbane, Brisbane's northern and southern suburbs, Townsville, Melbourne, the hills behind Noosa, and Sydney. Composed or compiled in the early years of her marriage, the poems printed in Section II exemplify Astley's happiest, as well as her bleakest, writing. Feelings of abandonment, loneliness and fear jostle with revelations of love fulfilled and of peace and security achieved – 'You are my quiet music' (124). Lyrical transpositions of Queensland seascapes and landscapes into traditional poetic forms. 'Magnetic' (105), 'Whitsunday' (131) and 'Picnic' (123) contrast with disenchanted examinations of city and suburban life that are indebted to T S Eliot – the *Prufrock* crab simile in 'Over the young backyards each day ...' (103) is an example. Technically sure-footed poems like 'Satori' (107) and 'Solvency' (125) further deepen the nature mysticism of Astley's schoolgirl poems.

Astley's much-discussed claim[85], made in 1985, that she had been 'neutered' by her upbringing in a misogynist culture, and that 'the only way one could have any sort of validity was to write as a male'[86], *i.e.* with the voice and from the perspective of male characters, overlooks her autobiographical first-person stories. These include 'Double Vision' (1963) and 'Coming of Age' (1966) as well as Gabby, the first-person female narrator of *An item from the late news* published in 1982.

Most significantly, the present selection demonstrates that Astley made generous use of a first-person speaker cognate with herself in the poetry that she wrote between 1939 and 1957. A suspicion that she may have revealed more than she intended may have been another reason why Astley left her poetry uncollected and largely unpublished at her death.

EDITOR'S BIOGRAPHY

Cheryl Taylor taught literature and effective writing at James Cook University for many years before retiring as an Associate Professor in 2006. Since moving to Brisbane's bayside, she has held teaching and research positions at Griffith University. She has edited books and published articles on Middle English and Medieval Latin literature and the literature of spirituality. Her publications on Australian literature, which include the editing of a regional subset within the *AustLit* database, have dealt mainly with Queensland writers.

EDITOR'S ACKNOWLEDGEMENTS

I am grateful for the Fryer Library Fellowship, 2010, that funded my study of Thea Astley's poetry archive in Fryer and elsewhere, to Vanessa Pellatt for helpful suggestions and careful checking of the editing process, and to the *AustLit* director, Kerry Kilner, who brought this project to the attention of the University of Queensland Press.

Cheryl Taylor

ENDNOTES

Introduction

1. Thea Astley in Ray Willbanks (ed.), *Australian Voices: Australian Writers and Their Work*, University of Texas Press, Texas, 1991, p. 37.

Section I: Childhood and Youth

Unless otherwise stated, the Endnotes to Section I record Astley's unsystematic dating and sourcing of individual poems in Exercise Book A.

2. University of Queensland Fryer Library 97/42.

3. Published *The Courier-Mail*, 4 January 1934, p. 8 when Astley was eight. Her father, Cecil Astley, was a sub-editor at the paper.

4. *All Hallows' magazine*, 1939, p. 40.

5. Individually dated by Astley to 1940; *All Hallows' magazine*, 1940, p. 38; republished Karen Lamb, *Thea Astley: inventing her own weather*, University of Queensland Press, St Lucia, 2015, p. 30.

6. Dated to 1941 by Astley.

7. Astley locates this unpublished poem in 'Warwick'. She probably wrote it when her All Hallows senior class was evacuated there in 1942 for fear of air raids.

8. *All Hallows' magazine*, 1942, p. 58.

9. *All Hallows' magazine*, 1943, p. 51.

10. ibid., p. 54.

11. Dated by Astley to 1943; *Barjai* 13, May 1944, p. 3; republished with subtitles omitted, Lamb, pp. 62–3.

12. 'To Laurie' is the first poem to fall under Astley's heading '1944' in Exercise Book A. Together with Barrie Reid, Laurence Collinson founded the *Barjai* group of young poets and artists in Brisbane in the early 1940s. *Barjai* means 'a meeting place for youth'. Astley's Fryer archive contains four poems addressed to Laurie.

13. *Barjai* 15, July 1944, p. 16. The texts in this edition reproduce Astley's manuscript punctuation, which places inverted commas at the beginning of each line of quoted speech, commas and stops before closing inverted commas, and stops after initials.

14. 'Creation' won the *Barjai* poetry competition judged by Clem Christesen, the founding editor of *Meanjin*, who at the time was a sub-editor with Astley's father on *The Courier-Mail*. Christesen commented: 'I have chosen Thea Astley's "Creation" as the most successful of the poems submitted. Allowing for its structural faults, I was impressed with its sincerity, its validity. Most of the poems were far too loose in form, lacking in emotional and mental content and discipline'. *Barjai* 15, July 1944, pp. 16–17.

15. *Barjai* 16, September–October 1944, p. 5.

16. *Galmahra*, 1944, p. 8.

17. Published *Barjai* 14, June 1944, p. 3 with the title 'To H'.

18. Dated by Astley to 14 July 1944; *All Hallows' magazine*, 1944, p. 39.

19. My best guess for the meaning of this title, which Astley seems to have invented, is 'sounds, noises' derived from such Latin words as *sono*: 'I sound' and *sonitus*: 'a sound, noise'.

20. *All Hallows' magazine*, 1944, p. 48. This is Astley's translation of Charles Baudelaire's sonnet 'Recueillement'.

21. *Barjai* 17, November–December 1944, p. 9; 'For the Pleasure of Thea', Collinson's response to Astley's poem, appeared in *Meanjin papers* Autumn Vol 3, No 1, 1944, p. 59. He exhorts Thea to 'Glide gallantly forward … realise that *you* are the only One to deify'.

22. Republished Lamb, p. 84.

23. Dated by Astley to Monday 11 December 1944.

24. Dated by Astley to December 1944.

25. *Barjai* 16, September–October 1944, p. 5.

26. *Galmahra*, 1944, p. 14; the epigram, *Alas, how they glide by, Postumus, Postumus, the swift years!*, is the opening to Horace's *Ode* 2.xiv, on human beings' subjection to time, old age and death.

27. *Barjai* 17, November–December 1944, p. 9; Exercise Book A does not contain a copy of this poem.

28. Dated by Astley to 15 January 1945; published *Barjai* 18, No. 1, 1945, p. 13 as the first of 'Two Poems'; republished Shelton Lea & Robert Harris, *A flash of life*, Christine Webb, Mountain View, Vic, 1986, p. 10; and Lamb, p. 78.

29. Astley's note locates this poem in Melbourne. It follows 'To My Brother' under the heading 'Two Poems' in *Barjai* 18, No. 1, 1945, p. 13; republished Lamb, p. 66.

30. Dated by Astley to 24 January 1945.

31. The placing of this poem in Exercise Book A confirms Astley's dating of its composition to January 1945.

32. Dated by Astley to March 1945.

33. Dated by Astley to April 1945.

34. *Galmahra*, 1945, p. 24; not held in Astley's Fryer Library archive.

35. ibid., p. 25; dated by Astley to May 1945.

36. *All Hallows' magazine*, 1945, p. 56.

37. ibid., 1945, p. 33.

38. *Barjai* 19, No. 2, 1945, p. 13.

39. *Après* seems to mean 'in imitation of Baudelaire's style'. This poem has some resemblance to Baudelaire's 'Chant d'Automne' part ii, No 311, in Astley's student copy of St John Lucas (ed.), *The Oxford book of French verse, XIIIth century–XXth century*, Clarendon Press, Oxford, 1942, p. 442.

40. Dated by Astley to June 1945.

41. Astley gives 27 October as this sonnet's completion date.

42. Dated by Astley to December 1945.

43. *Galmahra*, 1945, p. 25; republished Elizabeth Perkins and Robert Handicott (eds.), *North of Capricorn: an anthology of verse*, Foundation for Australian Literary Studies, James Cook University, Townsville, 1988, p. 5; and Lamb, p. 64.

44. *All Hallows' magazine*, 1945, p. 31; 'Ballad', which is not held in Astley's Fryer Library archive, selects stanzas from Victor Hugo's 'Un Peu de Musique', No 255 in Astley's student copy of *The Oxford book of French verse*, pp. 359–61.

45. This poem is written on a loose leaf inserted into Astley's copy of *The Oxford book of French verse* beside the original, Théophile Gautier's 'Chinoiserie', No 284, pp. 419–20. She published the poem in *All Hallows' magazine*, 1945, p. 31 under the title 'China Things (from Gautier)'.

46. Astley pencilled this translation in the right-hand margin of her *Oxford book of French verse* against the original, Paul Verlaine's 'Chanson d'Automne', No 317, p. 463.

47. Interview recorded by Suzanne Lunney, Canberra, 16 April 1974, NLA.

48. Astley notes this poem as based on Alfred de Musset.

49. Dated to Sunday 17 March and noted by Astley as based on Alfred de Musset.

50. *Barjai* 20, No. 1, 1946, p. 17.

Section II: Adulthood

Unless otherwise stated, the endnotes to Section II record the dates and places that Astley attributed to her poems in Exercise Book B.

51. University of Queensland Fryer Library 97/41.

52. Lamb, p. 99.

53. Dated by Astley to 1945.

54. Dated by Astley to 1946.

55. Dated by Astley to 1946. The family home of Cecil and Eileen Astley, and their children Philip and Thea, was at 358 Waterworks Road, Ashgrove. It is a pleasant, high-set house with a wooden lattice that in 2016 was still ensconced in gardens and maintained in its original Queensland style.

56. Attributed by Astley to 'Townsville 1947'. Astley taught at the Hermit Park and the Central State Primary Schools in Townsville, North Queensland, from January to August 1947. She first met Jack Gregson at a Brisbane chamber music concert in the August school holidays of that year. From August to December 1947 she taught at the Imbil State Primary School, west of Noosa.

57. Dated to 1947 by Astley, who notes that this poem was published in the *ABC Weekly*.

58. Dated by Astley to January 1948. The title probably refers to Echo Point lookout above the Albert River in Queensland's Lamington Park; Astley's financial and employment constraints seem to rule out the better-known Blue Mountains site.

59. Ascribed by Astley to 'Pomona 1948'. After resitting failed University of Queensland exams in November 1947, and thereby qualifying for her BA degree, in January 1948 Astley took up a secondary teaching post at Pomona Rural High in the Sunshine Coast hinterland.

60. Ascribed by Astley to 'Pomona, Wednesday, June 1948'.

61. Dated by Astley to May 1949.

62. Dated by Astley to 1949.

63. Dated by Astley to May 1950.

64. Dated by Astley to May 1950.

65. Dated by Astley to 1950.

66. Astley has printed the present title for this sonnet over a crossed-out earlier title, 'The Island'. The poem clearly refers to Magnetic Island eight kilometres from Townsville, which became an important reference point in Astley's novels, such as *Girl with a monkey* and *Coda*. Astley states that the sonnet was published in *The Sydney Morning Herald.* This is the first in Astley's series of typed, pasted-in and mostly undated poems in Exercise Book B.

67. As well as in Exercise Book B, this poem occurs late in A with the title 'Charles', under the general heading '1945'.

68. Exercise Book A contains a draft of this sonnet, attributed by Astley to 'de Musset', and, from its position in A, written in 1945. The closing line of the earlier draft reads: 'And only grim beyond, the waiting years'.

69. *The Sydney Morning Herald*, 19 October 1957, p. 12; republished Lamb, pp. 100–1. Lamb misreads the title, which appears in both Exercise Book B and the *SMH* as 'Sulpicia Ill', *i.e.* 'sick'. Astley as speaker is not identifying herself with an unrecorded third Roman poet named Sulpicia. Instead, she is claiming kinship with Sulpicia as representative of all female poets from classical times to the present. Punctuation follows the *SMH* text.

70. Published in *The Sydney Morning Herald*, 3 August 1957, p. 17.

71. A draft of this poem is pencilled on a separate page inserted into Exercise Book A. Astley parodies some lines in *Drylands: a book for the world's last reader*, Penguin, Ringwood, Victoria, 2000, p. 13.

72. This text incorporates small changes that Astley made to the later of the two versions of this poem in Exercise Book B. The earlier version, typed on a loose page inserted into B, gives her address as 44A Dorset Street Epping, where she lived with her husband and son from 1956 (see Lamb, photos following p. 178).

73. This poem was first published in *The Bulletin* Vol 75, No 3878, 9 June 1954, p. 13, with the title 'Piccaninny Thoughts'. Four subsequent printings – in A A Philips (ed.), *Australian Poetry 1956*, Angus and Robertson, Sydney, 1956, p. 52; R S Byrnes and Val Vallis (eds.), *The Queensland Centenary Anthology*, Longmans, London, Melbourne, 1959, p. 221; Douglas Stewart (ed.), *Modern Australian Verse*, Angus and Robertson, Sydney, 1964, pp. 176–7; and Perkins and Handicott, p. 6 – make 'Droving Man' Astley's most frequently anthologised poem. Her choice of the drover's wife as female focaliser nevertheless challenges the poem's traditional bush vocabulary and themes.

74. Published in *The Sydney Morning Herald*, 1 September 1956, p. 14, under the pseudonym Philip Cressy.

75. This poem is handwritten in Exercise Book B. The text is as Astley edited it later on a loose carbon copy inserted into the end of B. 'A Last Year's Hero' was published in *The Sydney Morning Herald*, 16 July 1957, p. 18, and in Hal Porter (ed.), *Australian Poetry 1957*, Angus and Robertson, Sydney, 1957, p. 15.

76. As the last poem written into the pages of Exercise Book B,

'The Purist' marks the end of Astley's discontinued attempt to compile a publishable collection. The text here follows the latest of three versions written on a loose page inserted into B. 'The Purist' was published in *The Sydney Morning Herald*, 7 September 1957, p. 15.

77. Not preserved in Astley's Fryer Library archive, 'Short Story' was published in Nan McDonald (ed.), *Australian Poetry 1953*, Angus and Robertson, Sydney, 1953, p. 48.

78. 'Cuckold', signed 'Philip Cressy' with 'Thea Astley' above, is handwritten on a loose page inserted into Exercise Book B.

79. J M Couper, Astley's colleague at Macquarie University from 1967, first published 'For You, Angela: Surfers' Paradise', his translation of Horace's *Odes* 1.v, in David Campbell (ed.), *Australian Poetry 1966*, Angus and Robertson, Sydney, 1966, p. 12. The manuscript for Astley's translation is a page torn from an exercise book (Fryer Library 97/44). She later added a heading: 'My version of Horace 1.v. J. M. Couper has done a lovely parodic version'. Her annotations show that she did not consider this poem finished. She wrote at the foot: 'It's not the best, Coup, but I didn't want to do a mod'. An arrow points from this comment to a note written against the last stanza: 'It's that double sea rhyme mucks it up!'

80. The text of Astley's 'Reply' follows the typed fair copy that accompanies her handwritten draft of this poem in Fryer Library 97/44 (c). Couper's 'Peter Abelard to Eloise' appears in his anthology *In from the Sea*, The Wentworth Press, Surry Hills, NSW, 1974, p. 16. Astley's annotation states that Couper's poem was published in *The Sydney Morning Herald*, and her reply may have appeared there too.

81. Two versions of this beautiful poem exist in Astley's Fryer Library archive. The typed version, printed first, is Astley's

fair copy of a pencilled and corrected draft on a group of loose leaves (Fryer Library 97/44 (d)). The second version, 'After Tasman', printed on the facing page, is based on a corrected draft pencilled on the middle page of an exercise book that otherwise contains mostly stories (Fryer Library 97/43). 'After Tasman' was published in *The Bulletin* Vol 83, No 4288, 21 April 1962, p. 60; and in Perkins and Handicott, p. 4. Janet quotes from it in *Drylands*, p. 13.

82. Thea Astley in Norma Jean Richey, 'An Interview with Thea Astley', *South Central Review* 3 (2), 1986, p. 100.

83. Thea Astley in Amanda Smith, 'Thea Astley: The Outspoken Writer Talks about Australian "Culture Cringe"', *Publishers' Weekly* 237.13, 1990, p. 43.

84. Thea Astley, *Drylands*, p. 199.

85. For example, Susan Lever, 'Ratbag Writers and Cranky Critics: In Their Praise', *Journal of the Association for the Study of Australian Literature* 4, 2005, p. 16.

86. Thea Astley in Candida Baker, *Yacker: Australian Writers Talk About Their Work*, Picador, Sydney, 1986, pp. 42–3. This interview took place in Canberra in March, 1985.

INDEX OF TITLES

A Last Year's Hero	133	Edward Street	74
A Seasonal Lament	134	Enchantment	16
A Warning	120	Fantasy	14
Absent	20	For the Pleasure of Laurie	41
After Tasman	143	Fragment	117
Altar Piece	62	From Troy	22
And again	68	Grey Afternoon	29
Ashgrove Hills	94	Horace 1. v	140
At the Seaside	10	Hunters Hill [1]	100
Ballad (translated from Hugo)	78	Hunters Hill [2]	101
Chinary	79	Idiot	26
Clown	70	Invocation	128
Creation	25	John	99
Culture, 1945	75	Juvenilia	85
Descant	132	Lament	118
Dreaming	12	Last Week	122
Droving Man	129	Letter to Nathalie	95
Dunes	121	Love in Our Time	126
Echo Point	97	Love's Fault	27

Lubra	130	Sonnet [6]	106
Magnetic	105	Sonnet: après Baudelaire	65
Meditation	40	Sonnet: Chance Meeting	38
Melbourne	54	Sonnet: Child by the Shore	33
Neap	108	Sonnet: Frustration	34
On hearing the first cuckold in		Sonnet: To Francis Thompson	35
spring	139	Sonnet: To Myself	36
Picnic	123	String Quartet	43
Poem [1]	24	Sulpicia Ill	115
Poem [2]	32	Summer	119
Poem [3]	47	The Awakening	15
Poem [4]	49	The Card Players	57
Poem [5]	53	The Purist	135
Poem [6]	124	The Sailor	61
Query	28	The Shadows	21
Rain after Drought	82	The Unwanted	63
Returned Man	60	To a Poet	69
Revelation	42	To Helen	37
Roland to Arlène	58	To Isa	46
Satori	107	To Laurie [1]	23
She	71	To Laurie [2]	67
Shorncliffe	56	To My Brother	52
Short Story	138	To You – The Poet	18
Solvency	125	Tomorrow	98
Song [1]	44	Toni's	64
Song [2]	48	Trellis	45
Sonites	39	Unrest	13
Sonnet [1]	50	Vignette	59
Sonnet [2]	66	Whitsunday	131
Sonnet [3]	72	With Evening	30
Sonnet [4]	73	Written in reply to J.M. Couper's	
Sonnet [5]	104	'Abelard to Eloise'	141

INDEX OF FIRST LINES

A woman sat beside me in the train,	32
All night during the wind	99
All through the month of August	138
All we regret, we singers in the sun,	85
Always and reasonably, it is sad	126
'Because perplexed me people's laughter, words	63
Be wise, O my Sorrow, and calmer tread your way.	40
Beyond the sleeping and the wake,	47
Beyond this year – the unknown corridor,	50
Boringly repetitive the night	53
Charmed like a moon-slaked orchard, here the streets	67
Charted your coast without once touching land	143
Christopher Robin hand in hand	10
Clean on the valley's edge of afternoon,	123
Enter – harshness,	42
Flesh-fettered so I plead to clasp the real	96
For three nights now we two have lain	132
Four fiddlers by the shaded lamp,	43

Futility appears the total day,   112

Grief is thin as the moon.   71

Half of my kith and less of my kin   115

'Hand me your hat and I will pour   122

He picked a rose   26

Here boredom works through plangency   134

His eyes were full of holy things.   61

How awkward just to offer thanks   68

I am torn between my soul and you,   65

I beg you, all might soon dissolve, but this,   114

I find no solace in the haunting days   13

I must be cursed by some black doom   102

I said:– 'O look at the trees!'   49

I shall remember though the years deny   97

I'll lean along the driving rain   127

If you like, let's make a dream   78

In acres and oceans bright green on blue wave bending   125

It is not you, fair lady, whom I love,   79

It's pleasant to dream and lie   12

'It's symbolistic, dear, that's what it is!   75

Lamp-flicker on the bending men   57

Landfall at night; the long seas took me in.   142

Last week the lugger's in   118

Let me plant a tune or buy a singing bird   92

Light this branch at the moon,   59

Limpid afternoon, water-light   29

'Look,' sang the boy,   24

Look! There is beauty lying here!   64

My dearest lady,   58

My room is patterned with leaves,   21

My thoughts have borne me far –   14

No more need these lips song-sue 110

No trees are witnesses, or she 101

Not yet have I stumbled upon a philosophy 27

O the gentleness on my soul 94

Only an hour or so my friend – then pass 37

Only monkish cant could turn 141

Over the young backyards each day, and I 103

Pale sky, unto thy heart let me be gathered 16

Play Hansel to my Gretel in this forest 128

Pyrrha, who's the slender fellow 140

Quick, love, snatch the curtains from the years, 48

She might have chosen cities, but the man 129

Silently let's pause beside the dawn 73

Sing of the sunset sky, the strange chill plains 22

Sleekly the marble holds them 62

So I said smiling quietly: See 120

Some spikenard 121

Sometimes, incredibly, the longing swings 104

Summer is sweetness 39

Sun-flash on water, perhaps a writhing fire 34

Sunlight and spires are strangely tangled 52

Surely the eyes smile often 83

Take back the day. 60

Taking the day as primal postulate, 107

Tell me dear, how long 28

The crouching houses turn their moon-splashed sides 56

The flesh can bear a hurt, eradicate 84

The girl stood where the wind 130

The little minutes run me home 69

The long long hours of afternoon 54

The sadly sobbing strings 80

The thin lights of each day's disguise recede. 106

The totals of his thought were colourless 135

The uphill street and casual tram, 74

These quiet houses, river-lost, tremble away 100

This brain once rich 95

This day has been a season out of place, 38

This is true Pentecost, this downward heat 131

This love has more of spirit than of flesh, 66

This might be finality, the aim 72

This must be part of my making – 25

Those plagal cadences lamenting 139

Those were the months we found the summer texture 113

Thoughts pointed to the pole-star of the mind 105

Three days behind full moon, 82

Through the translucency of rain 117

To everybody with due exceptions 70

To reconcile four seasons in a day! 93

Today's intensity lies dying 98

Under strange seas of sky to a stranger sea 33

Unloose the golden bars of dawn 15

We met (a quiet street) within the town today, 46

When I am dead and little blades of grass 41

When shivering roses fade in sleep, 44

Where wind wanders round the curtains, 45

With evening the city was lost in an ocean 30

Within the cage of bones the sullen 119

You are my quiet music, you 124

You are not here today so I must find 20

You are the one who many years before 36

You have a slow smile 23

You know now. I've not said. 111

You may be sure I know my neap   108

You of the heart and I   116

You stood apart from others – weaver of dreams,   18

You wore autumnally the wreathier wreath,   133

Your words have spun eternity – and did   35